Hurray for B.C.

Selected Cartoons from
The Sunday Best of B.C.

Johnny Hart

Foreword by Bill Mauldin

CORONET BOOKS
Hodder Fawcett Ltd., London

to Auls, Jack, Peter, Thornton and Wiley.
YOU KNOW WHO YOU ARE.
My thanks,
Johnny Hart

Copyright © 1964 by Publishers Newspaper
Syndicate
Copyright © 1958, 1959, 1960, 1961, 1962, 1963 by
Publishers Newspaper Syndicate
First published 1964 by Fawcett Publications Inc.,
New York
Coronet edition 1973
Second impression 1974

Printed and bound in Great Britain for
Coronet Books,
Hodder Fawcett Ltd,
St. Paul's House, Warwick Lane,
London, EC4P 4AH
by Hazell Watson & Viney Ltd,
Aylesbury, Bucks

ISBN 0 340 16879 X

For details as to other books by the same author,
please turn to the back of this book.

FOREWORD

B.C. is one of the most brilliant examples of what is generally considered, by Johnny Hart's younger fans, as the "new school" of comic strips. Actually, as his older fans know (and there are more of them than he might think), it is in a grand old tradition which goes all the way back to 1911 and the beginning of *Krazy Kat*. Or, if you want more recent examples, there are *Toonerville Folks* (1924), *Barnaby* (1942), and *Sad Sack,* of World War II vintage.

All of these strips had two things in common: they were extremely, deeply funny, and they appeared to have been drawn in great haste. It was generally assumed by their devoted readers that their creators were so exhausted by the time they had thought up the ideas that they had nothing left to put into the art work.

Not so. The easiest picture in the world to draw is a cluttered one. Comic artists who fill every square inch with detail are known as "rivet men" in the trade, from the fact that they put every rivet on every boiler. What does it matter if the hero is a little offside in the panel? Stick in a computing machine, with hundreds of dials, or a tree, with every leaf. Nothing dazzles the customers like drawing every leaf on a tree.

But place two unwashed cavemen against a horizontal line, which could be the top of a swamp or the bottom of an overcast, or against a sloping line which could be the side of a hill or the edge of a rainbow, and you'd better place them right.

Not that Johnny Hart neglects truly important details in his work. What comic artist ever before took the trouble to research the exact sound of a lightning bolt striking? Thanks to Hart, the world knows today that it is "ZOT!" The artist will never be the same, but mankind is richer for the knowledge. And there are probably fewer than 10,000 serious paleantologists on the entire face of the globe who don't incline their heads respectfully at the mention of Hart's name, because he is the man who put "GRONK!" into a dinosaur's mouth. What else could a dinosaur say? Still, it took someone to first realize it.

There will be those who disagree with all I've said. The beginning term at every art school is crowded with kids who think that if you paint both eyes on one side of a nose you're on your way to being Picasso. And now there will be hordes of beady-eyed youngsters who will think that by free-wheeling drawing they can imitate Johnny Hart.

There might be a very few who can approach his draftsmanship, but there will never be another wit like his. Maybe it's just as well. Two such brains might constitute a critical mass, and then *B.C.* would have been responsible for a new kind of nuclear explosion, as well as the pre-Neanderthal discovery of fire, the wheel, sex, philosophy, and poetic whimsy.

BILL MAULDIN

Curls. A Master of sarcastic wit.

The Girls. (sigh)

Peter. A self-styled genius. The world's first philosophical failure.

B. C. a humble, meek, kind, naive slob. A pleasant encounter for those who don't like encounters.

Clumsy Carp, a friendly, unassuming maladroit. An assiduous student of ichtheology.

Wiley, a superstitious poet with an aversion to water in any form.

Thor. Inventor, artist, ladies' man. The inventor of the wheel, and the comb.

PLOP

PLUNK

ZAP

FIFTY THOUSAND MILES LATER.

SMACK

SURE IS COLD FOR FISH STUDYING!

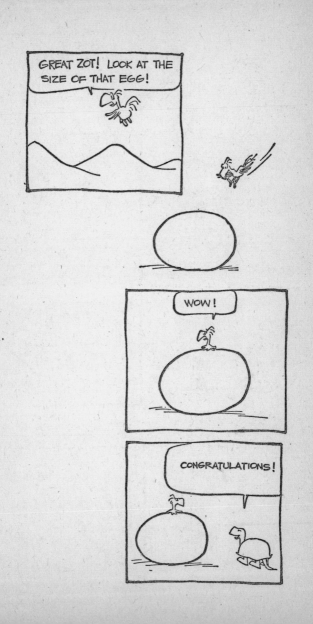

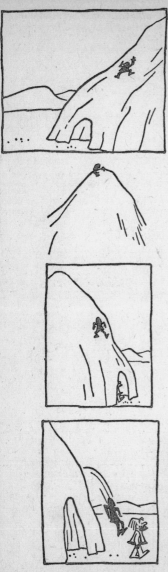

I GUESS IT'S JUST ONE
OF THE MYSTERIES
OF LIFE.

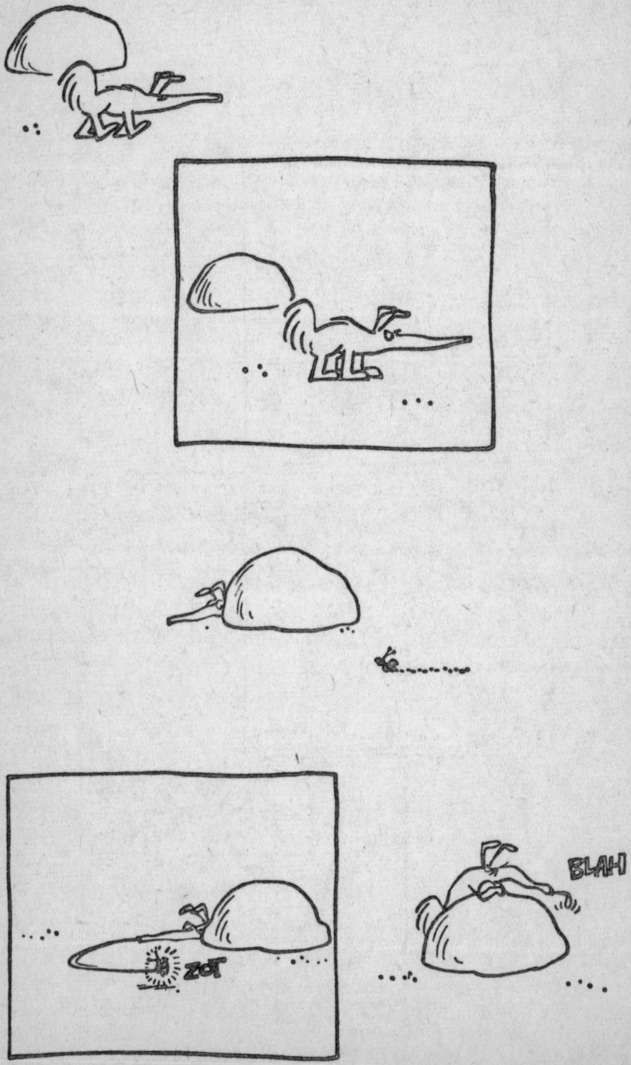
ZOT
BLAH

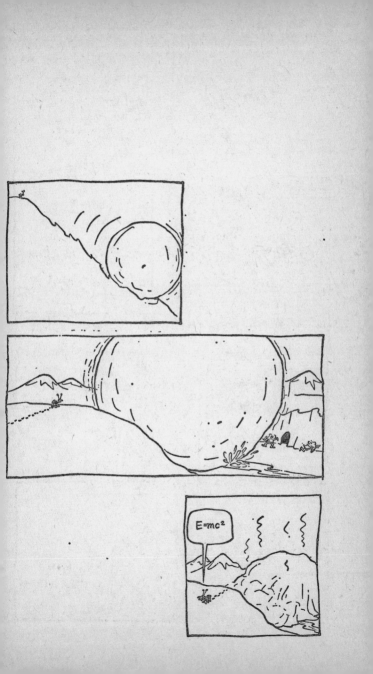

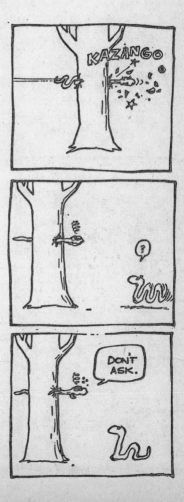

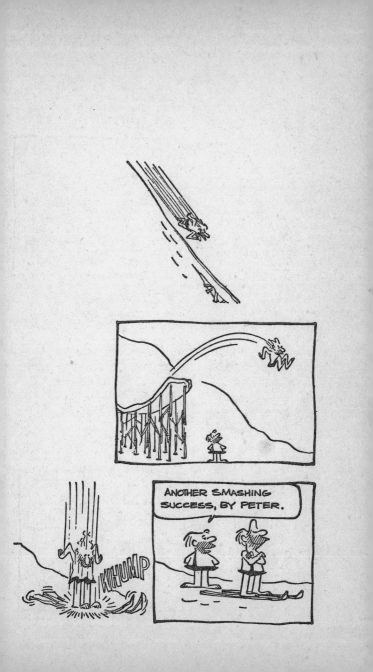

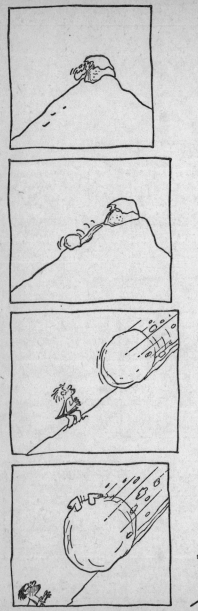

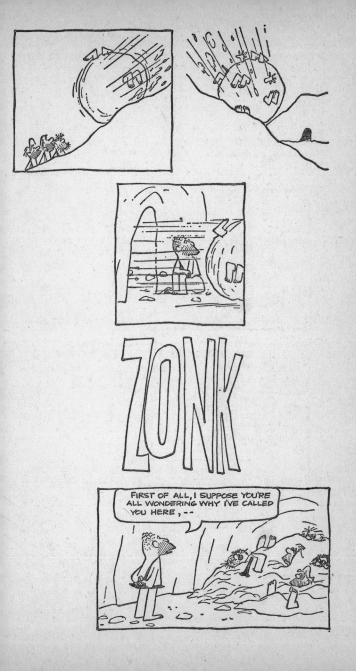

CHOP
CHOP
CHOP
CHOP

CHOP
CHOP
CHOP
CHOP
CHOP
CHOP

SOMETHING THAT BUGS
ME, IS A GUY THAT READS
OVER YOUR SHOULDER.

SHOULDER?

BLAAA

TOE GOT STUCK IN ONE OF THE LITTLE HOLES.

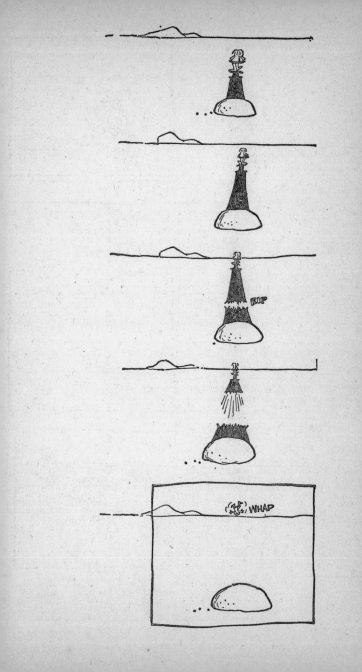

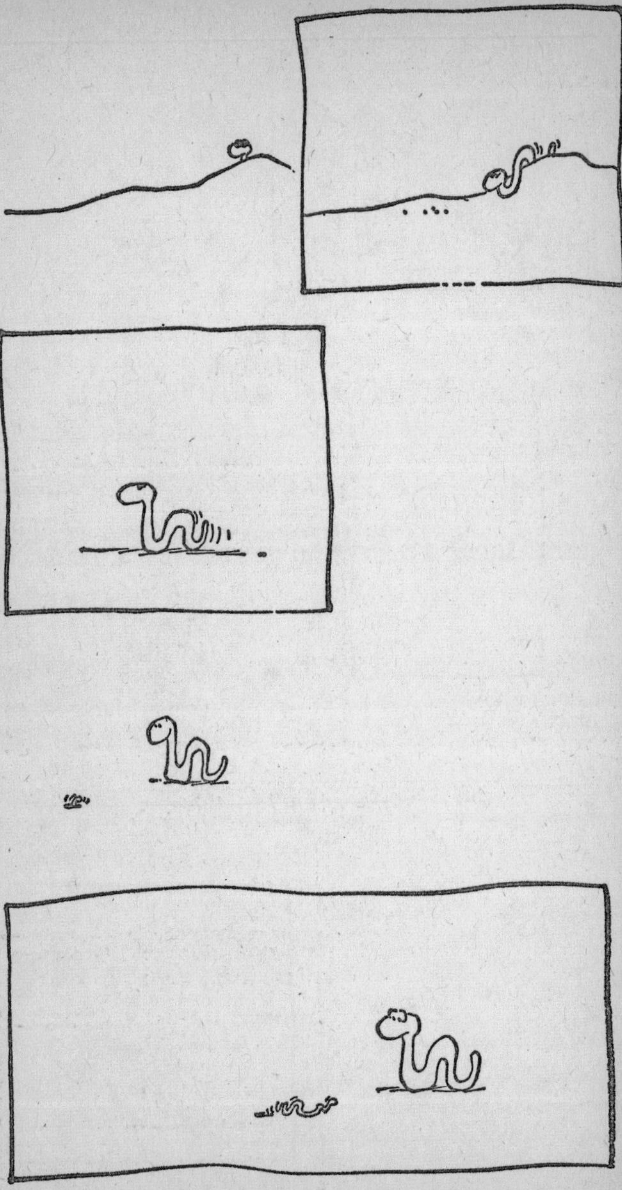

THERE, BUT FOR THE GRACE
OF GOD, GO I.

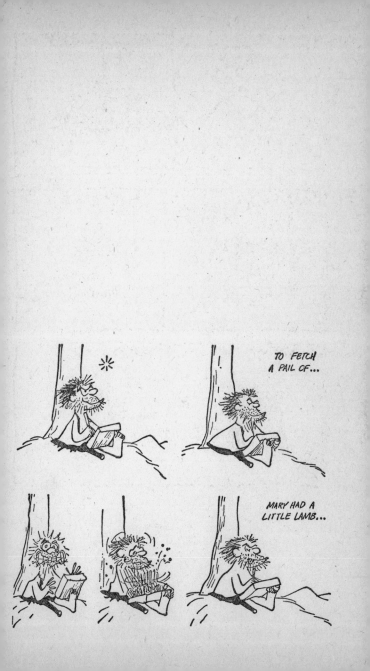

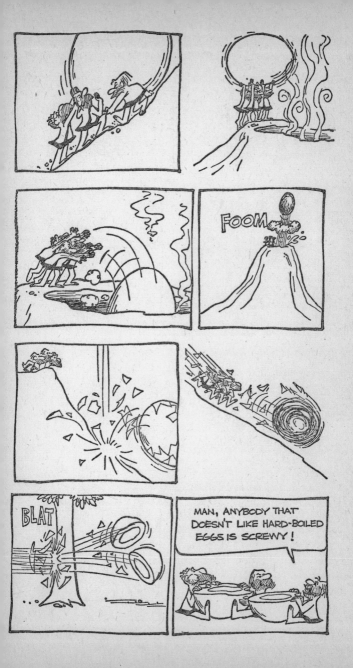

CORONET CARTOONS INCLUDE:

JOHNNY HART

☐	15694 5	Hey! B.C. (1)	25p
☐	15679 1	B.C. Strikes Back (2)	25p
☐	16477 8	Back to B.C. (3)	25p
☐	16881 1	What's New B.C.? (5)	25p
☐	16880 3	B.C. Big Wheel! (6)	25p
☐	18287 3	Take a Bow, B.C. (7)	25p

JOHNNY HART & BRANT PARKER

☐	15816 6	The King is a Fink (1)	25p
☐	15818 2	The Wondrous Wizard of Id (2)	25p
☐	16476 X	The Peasants Are Revolting (3)	25p
☐	16899 4	Remember The Golden Rule (4)	25p
☐	18604 6	There's A Fly in My Swill (5)	25p

CHARLES M. SCHULZ

Peanuts

☐	17844 2	Take It Easy, Charlie Brown (35)	25p
☐	17861 2	Who Was That Dog I Saw You With, Charlie Brown? (36)	25p
☐	18303 9	There's No-one Like You, Snoopy (37)	25p

GOSCINNY and UDERZO

☐	16054 3	Asterix the Gaul	25p
☐	16053 5	Asterix in Britain	25p
☐	16807 2	Asterix and Cleopatra	25p
☐	16806 4	Asterix the Gladiator	25p
☐	17656 3	Asterix the Legionary	25p
☐	17937 6	Asterix and the Big Fight	25p

All these books are available at your bookshop or newsagent, or can be ordered direct from the publisher. Just tick the titles you want and fill in the form below.

....

CORONET BOOKS, P.O. Box 11, Falmouth, Cornwall.

Please send cheque or postal order. No currency, and allow the following for postage and packing:

1 book – 10p, 2 books – 15p, 3 books – 20p, 4–5 books – 25p, 6–9 books – 4p per copy, 10–15 books – 2½p per copy, over 30 books free within the U.K.
Overseas – please allow 10p for the first book and 5p per copy for each additional book.

Name..

Address..

....